UNDERSTANDING RHETORIC

UNDERSTANDING RHETORIC

A Student Guide with Samples and Analysis

Elinor A. McNeel

UNDERSTANDING RHETORIC
A STUDENT GUIDE WITH SAMPLES AND ANALYSIS

iUniverse books may be ordered through booksellers or by contacting:

iUniverse
1663 Liberty Drive
Bloomington, IN 47403
www.iuniverse.com
1-800-Authors (1-800-288-4677)

ISBN: 978-1-5320-1697-4 (sc)
ISBN: 978-1-5320-1698-1 (e)

Library of Congress Control Number: 2017941804

Print information available on the last page.

iUniverse rev. date: 05/23/2017

CONTENTS

ACKNOWLEDGMENTS

I wish to personally thank the following individuals, without whose contributions to my inspiration, knowledge, and support this book would not have been written.

Cheryl P. Byrd, PhD
Clinical Psychologist

Holly Amber Gates, PhD
Penn State University, University Park

Kerry Ann Newman
Penn State University, University Park

Charlotte LaRae Washington
Rachel C. Sanders
Cynthia I. Coblentz

PREFACE TO STUDENTS AND INSTRUCTORS

People avoid writing because of the fear and anxiety they have about writing. Prior to attending Penn State and taking a rhetoric and composition class, I was one of those people. Depending on the style and the way the material is presented, you will find yourself creating essays and outlining speeches without giving it a second thought. After my very first English course at Penn State, I was over the fear and was not only able to pass the course with an A, but approached by my Effective Speech and Communications professor requesting my papers be used as samples in her upcoming courses.

A rhetorical situation, or, in short, rhetoric, refers to any set of circumstances that involves at least one person using a form of communication to modify the perspectives of another person. Rhetoric is the use of language, whether you are describing experiences or explaining concepts or perhaps sharing ideas. The writings in this book are designed to introduce your students to a variety of strong, well-organized, effective rhetorical strategies and tactics. The material is also suitable for any composition course pertaining to classroom writing projects.

I ask that you read and discuss in your classrooms the essays in this book and, hopefully, find subject matter that will motivate and improve the writer's skills in the following areas: rhetorical analysis, position arguments, proposals, understanding the rhetorical situation, and many more. Also included in this compilation are a couple of speeches, which I thoroughly enjoyed preparing.

Finally, as your students work through the discussion questions that follow the essays, the material will help them become more flexible and resourceful writers. The essays will also help them understand the purpose of reading and writing rhetorically, and how they will assist them in succeeding with your classroom assignments. The purpose for publishing these essays is so they may be used as supplements to writing workshops and tools for conversation in your everyday life.

ANALYSIS ESSAYS: INTRODUCTION

Analysis refers to the study of something to learn about its parts, what they do, and how they work together to create a whole. To analyze something is to make a critical assessment of it. The writer of an analysis essay will need to present and discuss relative merits and demerits, pros and cons, advantages and disadvantages, to analyze an idea or text or concept or another essay or research paper. It may also be necessary to present and discuss contrasting and conflicting findings with well-founded comparisons to present a clear picture about the topic. Finally, an analysis essay provides a conclusion to show the writer's preference or bias for a specific point of view.

Rhetorical Analysis

Free Speech and Free Tuition

On September 20, 2014, Barbara Garson, writer of the hit play *MacBird!* while at Berkeley, wrote an opinion article for the *Los Angeles Times* regarding her up-and-coming return to the University of Berkeley's fiftieth reunion of the Free Speech Movement that took place on its campus in 1964. Garson was active in the Free Speech Movement as editor of its newsletter.[1]

The University of Berkeley has a long-standing history for activism that goes back to the 1920s. In fact, during the early '20s there was a faculty revolt that secured for the Academic Senate an unprecedented role in shared governance of university affairs, which is still in effect today. Small student organizations at Berkeley, from the 1930s through the '50s, protested fascism and totalitarianism through peace strikes. In the late '50s students organized a campus political party, SLATE. The group was formed to promote the right for students to support off-campus issues. The university had a ban on activities surrounding on-campus political issues.

In 1964, the Free Speech Movement established a sit-in protest, which was the first of its kind. This particular protest was under the leadership of students Mario Savio, Michael Rossman, Brian Turner, Bettina Aptheker, Steve Weissman, Art Goldberg, and Jackie Goldberg, along with others unnamed. Among the Free Speech Movement activists were students who traveled with the Freedom Riders and worked with the Freedom Summer Project in Mississippi helping register African American voters. Over the years, the FSM changed its character. The fighting for rights demonstrations turned into parties, and now we had Haight-Ashbury, drugs, hippies, and rock and roll. The radicalization of the movement and the Vietnam War caused the character of the protests to change, and the demonstrations became violent. From 1967 to 1969, the police were using Mace to control crowds and students. My sister was attending UC–Berkeley at the time this occurred. She was leaving campus with a girlfriend after class and was tear-gassed along with other students outside Sather Gate as they crossed Telegraph Avenue.

Store owners offered warm, wet towels to students to place over their faces as they passed trying to escape the chaos. Huey P. Newton, a member of the Black Panther Party, was arrested for shooting a police officer. Outsiders began firebombing buildings, and the "Free Huey" movement began. This incident initiated another student demonstration, and hundreds were arrested while demanding the creation of a "Third World College." The People's Park demonstrations began shortly after the UC–Berkeley upheaval, which continued for more than a decade.

In her article, Garson mentions how surreal it would be for her to return to the same university that had nearly eight hundred students arrested in December 1964. She also recalls the experience they had with the forceful and controlling tactics the police used in trying to shut them up in the '60s, and how today there is a different kind of control over the students in the United States. It's referred to as economic control. Garson goes on to make a comparison between the cost of tuition in the '60s with today's cost of a college education. When she attended UC–Berkeley, her costs for a semester were $62.50, which included registration, healthcare, lab fees, and her student body card. Her tuition was free. Garson's rhetorical situation here is her not understanding, even with inflation, why tuition is what it is today. She explains that the increase couldn't possibly be for new stadiums or lavish buildings. She also disregards teachers' salaries as the cause. She states that "top academic administrative salaries, like top corporate executive salaries, have increased beyond inflation, it's true, but not by enough to account for a tuition increase from nothing to $12,000." During Lyndon Johnson's administration, grants allowed students with financial difficulties to acquire a college education. State and federal funds supported higher education in the '60s, but the wealthy rebelled against paying taxes, and government support came to an end.

Since 1986, overall inflation increased 115.06 percent (this is why we pay more than double for everything we buy). During this time, tuition increased 498.31 percent.

Schools have increased tuition fees due to higher overhead costs, and you have to consider that fuel and labor costs continue to rise. One of the main reasons tuition continues to rise is the change with Federal Stafford Loans. In 1992, the United States made it possible to access government-backed student loans without parent-income restrictions. The sudden influx of millions of additional aid dollars only further increased tuition. As the government continued its promotion for students to easily access massive amounts of money through Stafford Loans as a low-cost program, colleges followed their lead by increasing tuition rates. Garson makes reference to a relative who had a bad experience with student loans. The relative stayed home for six months with a new baby. While making arrangements with the lender to lower her monthly payments, she didn't realize her payment was being applied to interest, not principal. So, while her loans were in "forbearance" and she made monthly payments of $1,200 for fourteen years on an $80,000 loan, she now owes $93,000. Fortunately, at that time, this relative went straight through school without stopping until she acquired her PhD.

Garson refers back to reasons why she and a friend went to college. Their reason was, they thought, that they would be guaranteed the opportunity to earn a living. She now acknowledges that today's graduates are not afforded that same security. She looks forward to seeing old friends at the reunion—"along with nostalgia, I suspect we'll spend a lot of time wondering if there was something we should have done then, or could have been doing more of since then, to make things come out differently."

Comments and Questions

Who is the author/speaker?

- How does she establish ethos (personal credibility)?

- Does she come across as knowledgeable? Fair?

- Does the speaker's reputation convey a certain authority?

Understanding the Rhetorical Situation

Rhetorical Analysis of Ronald Reagan: 1986
Shuttle Challenger Tragedy Address

On January 28, 1986, Ronald Reagan was originally going to discuss the state of the Union—but instead the shuttle *Challenger* tragedy occurred, and his speech took another direction. The president identifies his audience in his opening address, "Ladies and Gentlemen, I'd planned to speak to you tonight to report on the state of the Union, but the events of earlier today have led me to change those plans."[1] He used the phrases "us" and "we," giving his audience a feeling of inclusion and involvement as he spoke. The speech was powerful, along with his deliverance, which left quite an impact on his television audience as they watched in horror as the shuttle exploded a few minutes after takeoff. Among the crew members killed in the tragedy was a schoolteacher, Christa McAuliffe. Her class, along with schoolchildren across the nation, witnessed the terrible accident on live television. As the president spoke, he reminded the children not to be discouraged, but to remember the crew as heroes and role models. The president wanted the children to know that sometimes in the process of exploration and discovery, tragedies can occur.

President Reagan's *Challenger* speech was delivered over national television. He spoke with emotion, resilience, and a display of grief as he mourned with our nation. He also displayed his own personal grief and compassion as he spoke to the families of the astronauts, at the same time telling them to continue to look to the future with faith. He was relaying a message to the public that we would continue moving forward with the space program and this tragedy would not diminish it. I found President Reagan's *Challenger* speech to be deliberative in that it seeks to influence thought and action; it also seeks to change policies and laws. When speaking to the schoolchildren, President Reagan encouraged them to not lose faith in the process of exploration and discovery and told them they should continue to be brave in their quest to expand their horizons. He reminded the children that we (America) were still pioneers, and that the members of the *Challenger* crew were pioneers with a hunger to explore the universe. This message was quite positive in encouraging the schoolchildren to not be discouraged by the tragedy that occurred that day, but to continue on with their hopes and dreams for a successful and rewarding future; it was also meant to convince the nation to look beyond the tragedy and see the fearlessness in the face of exploration by the crew members of never deserting the aim to achieve.

As we all know, President Reagan is known as "The Great Communicator." He earned this nickname because of his ability to convey his beliefs concerning economic and domestic policies to the public. His accomplishments while in office spoke for his credibility. "In Berlin, June 12, 1987, Ronald Reagan demanded, 'Mr. Gorbachev, tear down this wall!'"[2] He was well respected for his views on foreign policy, his devotion to defense, and the strengthening of our military. In an article written by Peter Beinart in the 2010 issue of Washingtonpost.Newsweek Interactive, LLC, additional accomplishments were mentioned regarding his toughness on terror and his ability to frighten the Soviet Union into submission.[3]

President Reagan and first lady Nancy Reagan flew to Houston to attend the memorial service at Johnson Space Center; he eulogized each of the seven members of the crew.

Notes

1. Ronald Reagan, "The Challenger Address," *The Ronald Reagan Presidential Library and Museum*, January 28, 1986, Accessed January 20, 2015. https://www.youtube.com/watch?v=vWPDNf9VMVo.

2. Newsweek Staff, "In Defense of Reagan," *Newsweek.com*, June 3, 1990, Accessed, January 20, 2015. http://www.newsweek.com/defense-reagan-206100.

3. Peter Beinart, "Think Again Ronald Reagan," *Foreign* Policy No. 180 (July/August, 2010): 28–33, Accessed, January 20, 2015. http://jstor.org/stable/20753961.

Comments and Questions

What is the rhetorical situation?

- What occasion gives rise to the need or opportunity for persuasion?

- What is the historical occasion that would give rise to the composition of this text?

POSITION ARGUMENT

The Positive and Negative Impacts of Cell Phones on People's Lives

What are the positive and negative effects of cell phones on individuals and society as a whole? Cell phones have become quite popular and have continued to become increasingly popular in the past years. Cell phones are considered a positive technological tool but in today's society, if used inappropriately, can become quite problematic. Some of the common factors considered today in cell phone use are the misinterpreting of text messages, driving while texting, and making phone calls while driving. We are all aware of the wide use of cell phones and its impact on our society, but the argument as to whether this issue is a positive or a negative one remains subject for debate.

The advantages of owning a cell phone are when situations such as an automobile accident, traveling, or a medical condition place a person in danger. With the assistance of direct and roaming cell phone coverage in practically all remote areas in the United States, having the convenience of a cell phone increases the ability for people to handle those emergency situations. It has been reported that well over half of cell phone users over the age of sixty-five have cell phone service for safety purposes. Owning a cell phone has become a vital tool for consumers, allowing users to search for discounts while shopping and purchase products directly from their devices. A US retail sales study conducted in 2010 showed $25 billion in growth through cell phone marketing. Small business owners can benefit through cost-effective ways in which to reach out to potential customers. Having access to a cell phone allows people to communicate with family and friends, and in case of a delayed meeting at one's business or place of employment, coworkers have the ability to not only reschedule meetings, but also coordinate and schedule reports or head off a crisis prior to the situation getting out of hand. The same basically goes for the smartphone, which also adds to the convenience of allowing one to check e-mail and send or receive important files domestically or internationally.

Additional advantages of owning a cell phone are its capabilities of helping those who are suffering from various disabilities, one being a vocal communication problem. For example, a person with autism now has the ability, through the cell phone's text and instant messaging functions, to speak using the text-to-speech feature without having to speak out loud. Smartphone owners can take advantage of applications such as word processing, calendars, mobile banking, web surfing, alarms, memos, video streaming, and games, to name a few. There has been a popularity explosion regarding applications for the iPhone, which allows users to download a large variety of apps from Apple's App Store. Cell phones also allow access to the Internet, help children with studies, and provide other simple functions such as the weather forecast or locating directions when traveling. Tracking devices are on some cell phones to assure parents or guardians of their child's whereabouts and safety. Children can use cell phones as a form of learning new technology—that is, exploring the Internet if it has the capability. Guidelines can be set by parents as far as teaching their older children to be responsible in always having their cell phone on hand in case of an emergency.

In contrast to the positive effects of cell phones, a recent study found that due to technology a new "connectedness" is being created by parents with their children, but as a consequence, old habits are disappearing. Internet browsing is replacing the once family activity of television watching as a group;

> While some families in the survey reported that 'family closeness' has actually increased with the advent of the Internet and cell phones, 60 percent said they think it has made no difference on their family's closeness (and 6 percent said it has had a negative impact). The study also suggests that the line has blurred between work and home thanks to the Internet and cell phones.

Before technology, families shared meals at the dining room table, discussing their days at work and school. People communicated with each other! Newspapers were read, and if there was something that needed researching, we went to the library. Technology has taken the place of in-person communication, and for that reason I believe it has become an issue. Now that we are in the information overload era and have become inundated with information from every source you could possibly think of, our behavior has become similar to that of drug addicts. Whether one chooses to face the facts or not, cell phone addiction exists. There may be someone in your group of friends or coworkers who is a cell phone addict, or it could be someone you know who sends text messages consistently, or that person who never turns his or her cell phone off for fear of missing a call. I have friends who have actually experienced anxiety attacks once they discover they have arrived at work and left their cell phone at home. I use my cell phone for emergency purposes only, so being without my phone all day at work has never been a problem. I have never been able to understand that kind of attachment to a cell phone. *See "The Growing Problem of Cell Phone Addiction" http://www.articlesbase.com/computers-articles/the-growing-problem-of-cell-phone-addiction-433680.html*.

Research has been performed on the effects of talking or texting on a cell phone while driving. The results of such use have not been proven, other than the fact that it is a distraction. The United States Department of Transportation and the National Highway Traffic Safety Administration (NHTSA) held two national "distracted driving" summits within the past few years. Cell phone use and texting have been banned for commercial drivers, and these agencies are encouraging all states to initiate tougher laws. Campaigns are being launched to raise our awareness regarding this issue. Nonetheless, the uncertainty of the research has not interfered with state governments taking this threat seriously. The NHTSA estimates that 25 percent of auto accidents are traced to driver distraction caused by the use of cell phones. An official US government website, Distraction.gov, reports that there were 3,328 distracted driving fatalities in 2012, and 421,000 people suffered injuries incurred as a result of motor vehicle accidents related to distracted driving. In the state of California, primary laws have been implemented regarding distracted driving, which permit police to pull the driver over. The fines are too lenient, in my estimation; they range from $50 to $100. I strongly feel that texting while driving should be a felony, whether an accident occurs or not, and the fines should range from $500 to $1,000, or more depending on the circumstances. Perhaps people would pay closer attention to the law and the possibility of taking their life, or the life of someone else.

In conclusion, it is inarguable that mobile phones are not perfect so far, but they can produce more valuable and beneficial influences. Cell phones save lives. As far as having immediate access in case of an emergency, a cell phone makes it possible for emergency responders to get to the injured or ill person much faster. Staying in touch with family and friends I feel are great benefits to owning a cell phone. On the other hand, the negative effects, such as texting while driving and not taking into consideration the fact that you are *not* the only person on the road, remain of great concern. My personal opinion is that all technology needs to and should continue to innovate; we simply need to reassess our behavior and become a little more structured in the use of technology, including cell phones. I strongly believe that the advantages outweigh the disadvantages as far as owning a cell phone.

Comments and Questions

What does the nature of the communication reveal about the culture that produced it?

- What kinds of values or customs would the people have that would produce this?

- How do the allusions, historical references, or kinds of words used place this in a certain time and location?

Global Warming: A Proposal to Increase Limits on Carbon Pollution

By Elinor A. McNeel

November 15, 2014

Executive Summary

Climate change is one of the most serious public health threats challenging our entire nation, and there are very few people who are aware of how it can affect them. It is also the single largest environmental and humanitarian crisis of our time. The Earth's atmosphere is overloaded with heat-trapping carbon dioxide, which threatens large-scale disruptions in the climate with disastrous consequences. This proposal is in support of a number of solutions, mainly the elimination of subsidies to fossil fuel companies, which can be implemented dependent upon our government agencies, and their ability to adhere to the effects of global warming and the changes presently affecting our climate.

Problem: Global Warming and Climate Change Due to Carbon Pollution

We are all aware of global warming, climate change, and the effects of carbon pollution, as this has been a national problem for quite some time now. Global warming is caused by greenhouse gases formed by high levels of carbon dioxide being emitted into the Earth's surface atmosphere. The burning of fossil fuel—that is, gasoline, coal, and natural gas—causes the rise of carbon dioxide and carbon monoxide and thus the increase in the Earth's surface temperatures, affecting humans, animals and plant life on Earth (Mukherjee).

There has been controversy as to whether global warming actually exists and whether the contributing factor is carbon dioxide, which is a derivative of fossil fuel.

> On June 23, 1988, Doctor James Hansen testified before a congressional committee that he believed with a 'high degree of confidence' that the greenhouse effect had already caused global warming. After that testimony, there has been an increasingly acrimonious debate between those who see the problem as the most serious one facing humans today and those who refuse to believe there is any problem at all. (Watts 1)

There are a number of man-made factors that contribute to global warming, such as oil spills from large ships and tankers transporting fuel across the globe, the inappropriate disposal of waste materials from chemical plants, and ground water contamination from sewage leaks. The process of fracking, which is the drilling for natural gas through underground water wells, is another environmental concern due to the chemicals used in the process. The main concern with this procedure is proper well design, and water handling procedures must be applied at every well.

Climate change has made a significant difference in the quality of air due to pollution. There are roughly thirty million Americans who suffer from asthma and other respiratory diseases due to unhealthy air pollution. The Environmental Protection Agency's Air Quality Index monitors data on a daily basis in order to alert people through a red or orange code system as to the level of ozone smog pollution on any given day.

Solution: Place Limits on Carbon Dioxide Pollution Spewed by Our Fossil Fuel Plants

There are a number of solutions that would help prevent or slow down global warming. Because of the amount of heat-trapping carbon dioxide, methane, and nitrous oxide in the atmosphere, it will take a number of different types of technologies and approaches to bring down the emissions of gases in our atmosphere. This proposal supports the best possible solution for setting the limits of global warming pollution and will attempt to eliminate subsidies to fossil fuel companies.

The phasing out of fossil fuel electricity is one solution that can be implemented by not building new coal-burning power plants, initiating a phased shutdown of coal plants—starting with the oldest and dirtiest—and capturing and storing carbon emissions from power plants (CHM). Transportation is another contributing factor to global warming. The government should consider the greening of transportation by improving efficiency (miles per gallon) in all modes of transportation. Also to be considered is the need to increase energy efficiency by switching to low-carbon fuel by building more Smart cars, rapid-transit transportation systems, light rails, bullet trains, and bus systems (IPS).

The course to be taken in order to accomplish the phasing out of fossil fuel electricity will be quite costly, to say the least, but will it pay off in the long run? The fact that our federal government spends roughly $11 billion yearly to support oil, gas, and coal industries makes one wonder. Subsidizing fossil fuel companies is a contributing factor to global warming, and our government is aware of the serious economic and social implications this country will suffer in the long run.

Another solution that must be taken into consideration is the use of nuclear power. Nuclear power has very few global warming emissions and is considered one of the alternatives to clean energy. The upside to nuclear power is the elimination of greenhouse gases, which frees us from the dependence of fossil fuel as an energy source. The downside to using nuclear power is the threat to our security, such as the possibility of an accident like the one the Fukushima Diaichi plant in Japan experienced.

Renewable energy sources such as solar, wind, geothermal, and bioenergy are available around the world. Renewable technologies are cost-effective and can create jobs in the process of reducing pollution. We should also take a closer look at our forestry and agriculture and what heat-trapping emissions are affecting. We can reduce emissions from deforestation and forest degradation by making our food production practices more sustainable (CHM). The use of "offsets" is an alternative for fossil fuel consumption, and is most commonly used for wind farms. Offsets are used in the reduction of emissions of carbon dioxide (i.e., greenhouse gases). This process is a temporary solution and is used only to offset the reduction of emissions of carbon dioxide (greenhouse gases), located in another area. The most common uses for offsets are wind farms, biomass energy, and hydroelectric dams.

Taking a closer look at energy efficiency technologies will allow less use of power to heat and cool our homes, businesses, and industries, which are our largest contributors to global warming. Unfortunately, it is going to take the efforts of more people like activist Chloe Maxmin, a junior at Harvard University who campaigned in 2012 for Harvard to divest its endowment from the fossil fuel industry. The university was investing large portions of its endowment in corporations that threaten our future and that of our planet.

Explanation of Reasons

The Group of Twenty (G20) is the premier forum for its members' international economic and decision making. Its membership comprises nineteen countries plus the European Union. The G20 leaders meet annually to discuss ways to strengthen the global economy, reform international financial institutions, improve financial regulation, and implement the key economic reforms that are needed in each member economy (G20).

An article written by David Roberts for *grist.org* discusses the events that took place five years ago at one of the G20 countries' meetings. At the meeting of the G20, the largest economies in the world pledged to phase out fossil fuel subsidies. Unfortunately, today the G20 countries are spending $88 billion a year subsidizing exploration for new fossil fuels. In a 2012 report from the Overseas Development Institute and Oil Change International (ODI), subsidies for production and use of fossil fuel globally were estimated at $775 billion. Contrary to the 2012 report, subsidies for renewable energy amounted to a mere $101 billion in 2013.

The article goes on to explain the different forms in which the investments come. There are three, to be exact. National governments are spending more than twice the amount spent by private companies searching for carbon fuels. The report's authors also point out that almost twice what the United Nations says would be required to provide universal global energy access. The United States piece of that subsidy pie was $5.1 billion.

Roberts goes on to explain the exacerbation of climate change: along with all of the additional problems fossil fuel develops, the public subsidy money is boosting fossil fuel exploration in areas where the market will not support it. "For every US dollar in renewable subsidies, there is US$2.5 invested in renewable energy, while a US dollar in fossil fuel subsidies only draws US$1.3 of investment."

Global CO_2 Budget

Global warming is driven by increases in atmospheric levels of greenhouse gases (GHGs), primarily carbon dioxide (CO_2) from the burning of fossil fuels. To a first approximation, the cumulative annual emissions over any particular period will determine the change in concentration, and therefore the amount of warming. This means that for any particular rise in temperature, there is a budget for emissions of greenhouse gases, including CO_2, which cannot be exceeded in order to avoid temperature rising above a target threshold. The higher the budget, the lower the likelihood of restricting warming to a particular level. This analysis focuses on budgets for CO_2 only—hereafter referred to as carbon budgets. (This is different from the UK government's carbon budget, which includes all greenhouse gases.) Each carbon budget is associated with a probability of not exceeding a particular temperature threshold. This reflects the degree of uncertainty that is inevitable when projecting such complex systems decades into the future.

The Climate Tracker Initiative Report shows that nowhere across the financial chain do players in the capital markets recognize, much less quantify, the possibility that governments will do what they say they intend to do on emissions, or some fraction of it. We noted how dysfunctional this is, and sketched what the players across the financial chain would have to do in order to deflate the growing carbon bubble, not least the regulators.

Clearly, governments need to put in place credible climate policies in the run-up to the finalization of a new global agreement in 2015 that shifts investor attention in a low-carbon direction. But this needs to be matched by reform of capital market frameworks to enable investors to read these long-term signals and take appropriate action. For each of the key conclusions of this report, we have identified specific recommendations for action over the next two years for policymakers, regulators, investors, and investment intermediaries (CTI).

Conclusion

The Clean Air Act calls for state, local, tribal, and federal governments to work in partnership to clean the air. We should convince national leadership to stop ignoring what the earth and scientists are telling us about global warming and climate change and instead start ignoring those who continue to deny it is happening. We must act now in order to adopt cleaner energy sources at home and abroad.

Works Cited

Climate Hot Map: Global Warming Effects around the World. Union of Concerned Scientists, 2011. Web. 14 Nov. 2014. http://www.climatehotmap.org/global-warming-solutions/.

G20 Australia 2014. (n.d.). Web. 15 Nov. 2014. http://www.G20.org.

Mukherjee, Bidisha. *Fossil Fuels and Global Warming.* 10 Jan. 2012. Web. 4 Nov. 2014. http://www.buzzle.com/articles/fossil-fuels-and-global-warming.html.

Overseas Development Institute and Oil Change International. (n.d.) Web. 15 Nov. 2014. http://www.odi.org/g20-fossil-fuel-subsidies.

Roberts, David. *Rich Countries are still Wasting Billions on Subsidies for Fossil Fuel.* 11 Nov. 2014. Web. 15 Nov. 2014. http://grist.org/author/david-roberts/.

Stapp, Kitty. *Opinion: The Pentagon Comes Up Short on Climate.* IPS News Agency. 2014. Web. 5 Nov. 2014. http://www.ipsnews.net/.

Unburnable Carbon 2013: Wasted Capital and Stranded Assets. Carbon Tracker Initiative. 2013. Web. 15 Nov. 2014. http://www.carbontracker.org.

Watts, Robert G., et al. *Global Warming and the Future of Earth.* Morgan & Claypool, 2007.

Comments and Questions

What is the content of the message?

- Can you summarize the main idea?

- What are the principal lines of reasoning or kinds of arguments used?

- What topics of invention are employed?

- How does the author or speaker appeal to reason? To emotion?

SPEECH: ORGANIZING AND OUTLINING

Global Warming: An Increase of Limits on Carbon Pollution

General Purpose: To inform.

Specific Purpose: I would like to inform my audience of the negative effects of global warming and solutions that may help solve this health threat.

Thesis: Climate change is one of our most serious public health threats, challenging our entire nation, and there are very few people who are aware of how it can affect them. I would like to share with you a number of solutions that may help solve this health threat.

Introduction

I.   [Attention Getter]: We are all aware of global warming, climate change and the effects of carbon pollution as it has been a national problem for quite some time now.

II. [Topic and Audience Adapt.]: The negative effects of global warming are a contributing factor to greenhouse gases. Greenhouse gases are formed by high levels of carbon dioxide, which are being emitted into the Earth's surface atmosphere. There is a threat to the survival of our civilization—we must act and act now.

III. [Establish Credibility]: I have performed extensive research on climate change and its negative effects, and hopefully the information I was able to gather will enlighten your views on how we should treat our environment and what we can do to prevent and/or limit the use of fossil fuel and its effect on humans, animals, and plant life on Earth.

IV. [Preview Main Points]: Through this speech I will first discuss how global warming is the single largest environmental and humanitarian crisis in our time; second, once we clearly understand the severe consequences of the effects of global warming, we can discuss our role in the solutions to this issue.

[Transition]: Let's begin by discussing the crisis of global warming.

Body

I. Despite overwhelming factual evidence, there has been political controversy as to whether global warming actually exists and whether or not the contributing factor is carbon dioxide, which is a derivative of fossil fuel. The main and most detrimental effect of global warming is the increase in the global average temperature, and our response to the issue has been far too slow.

A. Global warming is attributed to greenhouse gases formed by high levels of carbon dioxide being emitted into Earth's surface atmosphere.

   1. According to the article "Fossil Fuels and Global Warming" by Bidisha Mukherjee, in 2012, "The burning of fossil fuel, i.e., gasoline, coal, natural gas, etc. are all contributing factors which cause the rise of carbon dioxide and carbon monoxide causing the increase in the Earth's surface temperatures, which affects humans, animals and plant life on Earth."[1]

   2. According to the article "Global Warming and the Future of Earth" by Robert G. Watts, in 2007, "On June 23, 1988, Doctor James Hansen testified before a congressional committee that he believed with a 'high degree of confidence' that the greenhouse effect had already caused global warming. After that testimony, there has been an increasingly acrimonious debate between those who see the problem as the most serious one facing humans today and those who refuse to believe there is any problem at all."[2]

3. There are a number of additional man-made factors that contribute to global warming as well—for example, oil spills from large ships and tankers transporting fuel across the globe, the inappropriate disposal of waste materials from chemical plants, and ground water contamination from sewage leaks.

    a. According to the article "Oil and Gas Pollution" by the Water Pollution Lawyers: Flood Law Group, LLP, 2015, the process of fracking, which is drilling for natural gas through underground water wells, is another environmental concern due to the chemicals used in the process. The main concern with this procedure is proper well design, as well as ensuring water handling procedures are applied at every well.[6]

B. Climate change has made a significant difference in the quality of air due to pollution.

1. According to the article "8 Things We Hate About Summer Are Getting Worse with Climate Change" by the Natural Resources Defense Council (NRDC), in 2014, there are roughly 30 million Americans who suffered from asthma and other respiratory diseases due to unhealthy air pollution.[7]

2. The Environmental Protection Agency's Air Quality Index monitors data on a daily basis in order to alert people through a red or orange code system as to the level of ozone smog pollution on any given day.[7]

[Transition]: Now that you have an initial understanding of the problem, let's move on to my second main point: What can we be doing to work toward better solutions?

II. The good news is there are a number of solutions that would help prevent or slow down global warming.

A. Because of the amount of heat-trapping carbon dioxide, methane, and nitrous oxide in the atmosphere, it will take a number of different types of technologies and approaches to bring down emissions in our atmosphere.

1. According to the article "Climate Hot Map: Global Warming Effects around the World" by the Union of Concerned Scientists, in 2011, "The phasing out of fossil fuel electricity is one solution that can be implemented by not building new coal-burning power plants, initiating a phased shutdown of coal plants, starting with the oldest and dirtiest, and capturing and storing carbon emissions from power plants."[3]

   a. For example: A solution that must be taken into consideration would be the use of nuclear power. Nuclear power has very few global warming emissions and is considered one of the alternatives to clean energy. The upside to nuclear power is the elimination of greenhouse gases and freedom from our dependence on fossil fuel as an energy source. The downside to using nuclear power is the threat to our security, such as the possibility of an accident like the one the Fukushima Diaichi plant in Japan experienced.

   b. According to the article "World Energy Outlook 2014" by the International Energy Agency (IEA), "Overall coal use is expected to plateau and rise only very slowly after 2020. In this scenario, with coal use declining in the US, Europe, and China, India is actually expected to surpass the US and become the second largest coal consumer toward the end of this decade."[8]

2. Second, "Transportation is another contributing factor to global warming. The government should consider the greening of transportation by improving efficiency (miles per gallon) in all modes of transportation."[4]

   a. Today, many vehicles produced by US auto manufacturers are flexible fuel vehicles (FFVs), which can run on E85 (85 percent ethanol, 15 percent gasoline) and other ethanol-gasoline blends. Fuel-efficient plug-in electric (PHEV), hybrid, and alternative fuel vehicles are being sold now and could cut your fuel costs and help the environment. Also, fuel-efficient cars and trucks are also being sold now. If you consider a plug-in hybrid electric or an all-electric vehicle, charging stations for electric vehicles are increasingly available throughout the country.

b. "Also to be considered is the need to increase energy efficiency by switching to low-carbon fuel by building more Smart cars, rapid transit transportation systems, light rails, bullet trains, and bus systems."[4]

3. Third, renewable energy sources such as solar, wind, geothermal, and bioenergy are available around the world.

a. "Renewable technologies are cost-effective and can create jobs in the process of reducing pollution. We should also take a closer look at our forestry and agriculture. We can reduce emissions from deforestation and forest degradation by making our food production practices more sustainable."[5]

i. The use of "offsets" is an alternative for fossil fuel consumption and is most commonly used for wind farms. Offsets are used in the reduction of emissions of carbon dioxide (i.e. greenhouse gases). This process is a temporary solution and is used only to offset the reduction of emissions of carbon dioxide (greenhouse gases) located in another area.

ii. The most common uses for offsets are wind farms, biomass energy, and hydroelectric dams.

B. Phasing out fossil fuel electricity will be quite costly, to say the least, but will it pay off in the long run?

1. Consider that our federal government spends roughly $11 billion yearly to support oil, gas, and coal industries.

a. In Naomi Klein's book *This Changes Everything: Capitalism vs. the Climate*, she states, "If the world's ten biggest military spenders cut 25 percent of their defense budgets, it would free up an additional $325 billion to spend on green infrastructure every year."

b. Suggestions for improvement going forward would be to challenge the strategies of companies who are using shareholder funds to develop high-cost fossil fuel projects; review the cash deployment of companies whose strategy is to continue investing in exploring for and developing more fossil fuels and seek its return; reduce holdings in carbon intensive companies and use rebalanced, carbon-adjusted indices as performance benchmarks; and redistribute funds to alternative opportunities aligned with climate stability.

2. Subsidizing fossil fuel companies is a contributing factor to global warming, and our government is aware of the serious economic and social implications this country will suffer in the long run.

[Transition]: There are a number of effects of and solutions to the problems of global warming that would have been too lengthy to address in this speech. Hopefully, our government and you as a concerned individual will adhere to these solutions, mainly the elimination of subsidies to fossil fuel companies.

Conclusion

I. [Signal End]: In conclusion, as global warming continues to become more pronounced and the average global temperatures continue to rise, our environment will be an increasing threat to the survival of our civilization.

II. [Review Main Points]: Firstly, the rise of global average temperatures in the atmosphere and the effects of carbon pollution have been a national problem for quite some time. Secondly, the majority of the effects on global warming and climate change addressed in my research are caused by carbon pollution.

III. [Final Appeal]: The US Environmental Protection Agency's Clean Air Act calls for state, local, tribal, and federal governments to work in partnership to clean the air. We should convince national leadership to stop ignoring what the earth and scientists are telling us about global warming and climate change, and instead start ignoring those who continue to deny it is happening. We must act now in order to adopt cleaner energy sources at home and abroad.

IV. [Artistic Last Line / Closure]: Now that we are aware of some of the causes, effects, and solutions of global warming, let's do our part in taking steps to reduce energy use, improve efficiency, and help end global warming.

Notes

1. Bidisha Mukherjee, "Fossil Fuels and Global Warming," January 10, 2012, Accessed February 12, 2015, http://www.buzzle.com/articles/fossil-fuels-and-global-warming.html.

2. Robert G. Watts, et al. "Global Warming and the Future of Earth," Morgan & Claypool, 2007, Accessed February 15, 2015, http://www.morganclaypool.com.

3. "Climate Hot Map: Global Warming Effects around the World," Union of Concerned Scientists. 2011, Accessed February 14, 2014, http://www.climatehotmap.org/global-warming-solutions/.

4. Eric Bonds, "Opinion: The Pentagon Comes Up Short on Climate," IPS News Agency. 2014, Accessed February 12, 2015, http://www.ipsnews.net/.

5. "Climate Hot Map: Global Warming Effects around the World." Union of Concerned Scientists. 2011. Accessed February 14, 2014. http://www.climatehotmap.org/global-warming-solutions/.

6. Water Pollution Lawyers, Flood Law Group, LLP, "Oil and Gas Pollution," Accessed March 20, 2015, http://www.waterpollutionlawyers.com/oil-gas/.

7. Natural Resources Defense Council (NRDC), "8 Things We Hate About Summer are Getting Worse with Climate Change," July 1, 2014, Accessed March 20, 2015, http://www.nrdc.org/.

8. International Energy Agency (IEA) "World Energy Outlook 2014," November 12, 2014, Accessed March 22, 2015, http://www.iea.org/newsroomandevents/pressreleases/2014/november/signs-of-stress-must-not-be-ignored-iea-warns-in-its-new-world-energy-outlook.html.

Comments and Questions

What is his/her intention in speaking?

- To attack or defend?

- To exhort or dissuade from certain action?

- To praise or blame?

- To teach, to delight, or to persuade?

Speech: Outline and Bibliography

Hillary Clinton: Women's Rights Are Human Rights

General Purpose: To inform.

Specific Purpose: To inform the audience of the atrocities being committed against women worldwide through a speech given by Hillary Clinton in Beijing, China.

Thesis: On September 5, 1995, Hillary Clinton delivered a speech at the United Nations Fourth World Conference on Women in Beijing, China, to encourage the empowerment of women worldwide in regard to decision making, violence against women, poverty, and, above all, the separation, or lack thereof, of women's rights and human rights.

Intro

I. [Attention Getter]: "It is a violation of human rights when babies are denied food, or drowned, or suffocated, or their spines broken, simply because they are girls. It is a violation of human rights when women are doused with gasoline, set on fire, and burned to death because their marriage dowries are deemed too small ..."

These words were so eloquently delivered to the convention and to the nation by Hillary Clinton, who had catalogued a litany of barbaric and egregious abuses that were inflicted upon women around the world today and criticized China for seeking to limit free and open discussion of women's issues.

II. [Topic and Audience Adapt.]: Analysis of Hillary Rodham Clinton's "Women's Rights Are Human Rights" Speech in Beijing, China, 1995.

III. [Establish Credibility]: The research performed and the information I have gathered on human rights and women's rights will hopefully enlighten your views on this historic event that took place in Beijing, China, on September 5, 1995.

IV. [Preview Main Points]: Today I would like to discuss with you the speech that laid the foundation to give a voice to women who were forced to remain silent. I will be analyzing the four parts of the rhetorical situation, which are occasion, audience, speaker, and speech.

[Transition]: Let's begin by discussing this inhumane crisis occurring worldwide today.

Body

I. The occasion for Hillary Clinton's speech was a call to action regarding women's rights and human rights. As a lifelong advocate of women and girls' empowerment who has devoted most of her life to public service, the speaker explained how the challenge of this conference was to give voice to women whose experiences had gone unnoticed and unheard, and how one group of people's human rights are still being denied in many parts of the world.

A. Clinton's speech was meant to encourage the empowerment of women worldwide in regard to decision making, violence against women, poverty, and above all the separation, or lack thereof, of women's rights and human rights. Initially, Clinton's reason for delivering this speech in Beijing was to stand up against the Chinese government for their lack of human rights and women's rights.

1. According to the article "Remarks to the U.N. 4th World Conference on Women Plenary Session" by Michael E. Eidenmuller, in 2012, "The goals and greater challenge for this speech was to give voice to women everywhere, to strengthen families and societies by empowering women to take greater control over their own destinies, which cannot be fully achieved unless all governments, here and around the world, accept their responsibility to protect and promote internationally recognized human rights."[1]

2. According to the article "Hillary Clinton in China, Details Abuse of Women" by Patrick E. Tyler, in 1995, "A number of delegates, including exiles from Tibet and leaders from Taiwan, were denied visas to attend this meeting and a parallel gathering of private women's organizations. Ordinary Chinese citizens did not see or hear Mrs. Clinton's speech, which was blacked out on official radio and television."[3]

B. Thousands of Chinese women who were interested in attending these sessions simply had no opportunity to apply or gain access to the gathering.

1. There were five thousand Chinese delegates, all selected by the Communist Party and all with strong ties to the party or the government. Others were restricted from even coming near the conference site.

2. The news was limited to a carefully scripted menu, featuring a blizzard of enthusiastic propaganda on the enormous progress of Chinese women under the party's guidance. "The senior party official in attendance, Chen Muhua, refused later to take any questions on the speech. 'I'm sorry, I'm very busy,' she said. The official Chinese press was under instructions to ignore Mrs. Clinton's remarks until an official reaction had been considered."[4]

[Transition]: Now that we have established Clinton's reason for the occasion, let's move on to discuss her audience.

II. Clinton delivered her speech to all women worldwide. She paid special tribute to Director General Tikayev and Ms. Wyden, along with other ministers, ambassadors, excellencies, and UN partners.

A. The primary audience for this speech was governments and organizations that held the power to make her goal on the progress of women's rights possible.

1. This speech was for all women in our lives and the appalling things women have had to put up with—for example, rape, abortion, burning, and honor killings.

2. Clinton's eight statements begin with "It is a violation of human rights": "It is a violation of human rights when young girls are brutalized by the painful and degrading practice of genital mutilation. It is a violation of human rights when women are denied the right to plan their own families, and that includes being forced to have abortions or being sterilized against their will." She paints a very graphic and visual picture to her audience.

B. The second audience of this speech was the LGBT community.

1. The first issue Clinton addressed was how, when the United Nations passed the Universal Declaration of Human Rights in 1948, "the governments were not thinking about how it applied to the LGBT community. And how the rights were not applied to indigenous people, children, or people with disabilities, or other marginalized groups."[5]

    a. The second issue she raised was the question as to whether homosexuality comes from a certain part of the world. Some believe it is from the Western region of the world, and people outside the West therefore reject it. Gay people are a part of every society in the world. Clinton went on to discuss how members of these groups are entitled to dignity and rights because they share a common humanity.

    b. According to the 2011 article "Hillary Clinton: Being Gay is not a Western Invention, but a Human Reality" by Stephen Gray, the third issue Clinton felt was the most challenging was when people cite religious or cultural values as a reason to violate or not protect the human rights of LGBT citizens. Clinton stated in her speech delivered to a United Nations summit in Geneva, "Being gay is not a Western invention; it is a human reality."[6] She went on to name countries, such as South Africa, where the constitution protects the equality of all citizens, including gay people. Colombia, Argentina, Mongolia, and Nepal all have had equal rights applied to their LGBT citizens through Supreme Court rulings.

[Transition]: Hillary Clinton's speech was referenced as an example of great public speaking; it was said to be persuasive, informative, and interesting.

I. Hillary Clinton's "Women's Rights Are Human Rights" is an example of a great oration and clear dialogue.

A. The speaker is known for this famous speech, which is famed for its powers of verbal communication—making good use of the words and language to illustrate its subject matter.

    1. During Clinton's powerful speech delivered during the Women in the World summit in Manhattan, New York, she recalled her most famous speech in Beijing, when she declared, "Women's rights are human rights." This speech was the first delivered after her announcement that she was heading for the White House.[7]

    2. "Whether this address can be described in the category of powerful, persuasive, motivational, or inspirational speeches, the excellent powers of oration which are used makes it a famous speech."[8]

[Transition]: Those who worked on the Beijing speech saw a woman who, under intense scrutiny and pressure, was willing to gamble for a cause and principle she cared about.[9]

II. The speaker's goal was to spur the development of women in society, bring attention to the atrocities committed against women, and seek institution change.[2]

B. The speaker faced constraints regarding her speech prior to her trip to China from administration officials and politicians from both parties. They warned her that her presence there would put too much at stake regarding the administration's political agenda.

    1. Many Democrats and the State Department had their concerns. The concern was whether she would divert attention from foreign policy priorities. Leading Republicans in Congress were also opposed. Phil Gramm labeled the conference "an unsanctioned festival of anti-family, anti-American sentiment."

    2. The conference had international concerns as well. The Vatican was concerned about the platform on abortion and Islamic countries'

objections to the women's rights agenda. On the other hand, China was had a problem with the fact that they wanted the international attention of the global conference they were about to host, but they had no control over what Hillary Clinton was going to say.

3. Meantime, the president and first lady spoke publically against the Republican rhetoric that the conference would be anti-family and assured the Chinese that the United States wasn't sending a radical delegation to Beijing.

[Transition]: Hillary Clinton's speech resonated worldwide, and the famous line she uses, "Human rights are women's rights and women's rights are human rights, once and for all," is still a mantra today.

Conclusion

I. [Signal End]: In closing, I hope that I have been able to provide insight to the message Hillary Clinton delivered to women and to the world. Her intent was to use her platform as first lady to speak out for millions who couldn't speak out for themselves. Today, most people remember Beijing as Hillary Clinton's first major step in a long career spent advocating for women and girls.

II. [Review Main Points]: Hillary Clinton's initial intent for this speech was to stand up against the Chinese government for their lack of human rights and women's rights. Her speech reverberated around the world; she was criticized by the editorials beforehand and praised afterward. She stated, "I just want to push the envelope as far as I can on women's rights and human rights." She took big risks—and they paid off.

III. [Final Appeal]: Allow me to share a quote from the speech that was meant to spur the development of women in society: "Now is the time to act on behalf of women everywhere. If we take bold steps to better the lives of women, we will be taking bold steps to better the lives of children and families too."

IV. [Artistic Last Line / Closure]: Hillary Clinton stated, "We need to understand that there is no formula for how women should lead their lives. That is why we must respect the choices that each woman makes for herself and her family. Every woman deserves the chance to realize her God-given potential."

Notes

1. Michael E. Eidenmuller, "Remarks at the U.N. 4th World Conference on Women Plenary Session, Beijing, China," September 5, 1994, accessed April 15, 2015. http://www.americanrhetoric.com/speeches/hillaryclintonbeijingspeech.htm.

2. Ibid.

3. Patrick E. Tyler, "Hillary Clinton, in China, Details Abuse of Women," *New York Times,* September 6, 1995, accessed April 15, 2015. http://www.nytimes.com/1995/09/06/world/hillary-clinton-in-china-details-abuse-of-women.html.

4. Ibid.

5. Stephen Gray, "Being gay is not a western invention, but a human reality," *Pink News,* December 7, 2011, accessed April 14, 2015. http://www.pinknews.co.uk/2011/12/07/hillary-clinton-being-gay-is-not-a-western-invention-but-a-human-reality/.

6. The United Nations, "The Universal Declaration of Human Rights," December 10, 1948, Accessed April 21, 2015, accessed April 13, 2015. http://www.un.org/en/documents/udhr/.

7. Famous Women Speeches, "Speeches by Famous Women," PowerfulWords.info, June 2014, accessed April 25, 2015. http://www.powerfulwords.info/speeches/Hillary-Clinton/index.htm.

8. Ibid.

9. Lissa Muscatine, "Hillary Clinton is not 'calculating' or risk-averse. I watched her take a huge gamble—and it paid off," *Washington Post,* April 25, 2015, accessed April 25, 2015. http://www.washingtonpost.com/posteverything/wp/2015/04/25/hillary-clinton-is-not-calculating-or-risk-averse-i-watched-her-take-a-huge-gamble-and-it-paid-off/.

Comments and Questions

What is the form in which it is conveyed?

- What is the structure of the communication? How is it arranged?

- What oral or literary genre is it following?

- What figures of speech (schemes and tropes) are used?

- What kind of style and tone is used, and for what purpose?

SAMPLES: COMPLETED ASSIGNMENTS FOR REVIEW

Rhetorical Criticism

1. Briefly research the background of the speaker. Did the speaker establish a positive ethos in this address? In what way was the speaker qualified to speak on this topic?

   Mary Fisher, daughter of the wealthy and powerful Republican fundraiser Max Fisher, delivered the speech A Whisper of AIDS on August 19, 1992, to the Republican National Convention in Houston, Texas. Ms. Fisher established a positive ethos in her address by acknowledging that her second husband gave her the disease, but not once accusing or blaming him. Her emphasis was on the urgency of awareness and to change the views of the American public. "She also establishes credibility by telling her audience in paragraph one, 'I want your attention, not your applause.'"[1]

2. Who was the audience for this address? What common traits did the audience share? In what way did the speaker adapt the speech to this particular audience?

   Mary Fisher's audience for this address was the members of the Republican National Convention and the American public as she stated, "Tonight, I represent an AIDS community whose members have been reluctantly drafted from every segment of American society." She also appealed to the audience by using President Bush Sr. and his family to persuade the audience. "In the place of judgment, they have shown affection." Ms. Fisher showed how the president and his family were treating her like any other person and not shunning her, and that no one with HIV or AIDS should be treated differently than they were before they were diagnosed.[1]

3. What was the occasion of this address? To answer this question, research the public attitudes and beliefs about the subject matter of this speech at the time it was delivered.

The occasion of this address was to advocate HIV/AIDS education, prevention, and awareness. Mary Fisher, three months prior to this speech in Salt Lake City at platform hearings, addressed the Republican Party to lift the silence that had been draped over the issue of HIV and AIDS:

BACKGROUND. We examined the relationship between workplace AIDS education efforts and workers' knowledge about HIV transmission and their attitudes toward coworkers with AIDS. METHODS. Questionnaires were mailed to corporate and public service workers at 12 work sites to ascertain the extent of their knowledge about AIDS and their attitudes toward coworkers with AIDS. Each work site had offered an AIDS education program. The average response rate was 40%; 3460 workers returned questionnaires. RESULTS. Respondents' knowledge was largely consistent with available scientific evidence. However, a substantial minority still believe HIV infection can be transmitted through casual contact. Over 30% endorse the screening of new employees for AIDS, and 23% would fear contagion from an infected coworker. Thirty percent of the respondents expressed skepticism about the veracity of information from government sources and the scientific community. Work site comparisons show that where educational programs are minimal, employees know less about HIV transmission and hold more negative attitudes. CONCLUSION. Comprehensive workplace AIDS education programs can reinforce workers' knowledge about HIV transmission, thereby fostering more favorable views toward coworkers with AIDS.[2]

4. What was the purpose of this speech? Do you believe the speaker achieved this purpose?

The purpose of this speech was to make the public aware of the stereotypes and misconceptions of the disease, and that funding and research was at a standstill. She also wanted people to understand that HIV and AIDS was not just a homosexual disease, nor was it a disease that just infected prostitutes and intravenous drug abusers. Ms. Fisher's words changed public policy that night at the Republican National Convention in Houston, Texas.

5. What types of supporting material and reasoning did the speaker use in this address? Provide examples from the speech of the types you find. Did the speaker commit any fallacies? If so, identify them and provide an example of each from the speech.

    Mary referenced her father and how he devoted much of his lifetime guarding against another Holocaust. She stated, "He is part of the generation who heard Pastor Neimoller come out of the Nazi death camps to say, 'They came after the Jews, and I was not a Jew, so I did not protest. They came after the trade unionists, and I was not a trade unionist, so I did not protest. Then they came after the Roman Catholics, and I was not a Roman Catholic, so I did not protest. Then they came after me. And there was no one left to protest.'"[1]

    Mary Fisher appealed to her audience's emotions through fear and guilt. She appealed to fear as she personified AIDS as a killer that knew where you lived and where you liked to hide; she then appealed to guilt by moving the audience to feel responsible for not speaking out against the prejudices that prevent a cure for the disease. She let her audience know that "we are the ones capable of changing public policy."[1]

6. What cultural values and beliefs did the speaker appeal to in the address? Provide examples from the speech to support your observations.

    Mary Fisher wanted her audience to understand and grasp her vulnerability; she wanted them to understand that she lived the "conservative, white picket fence, two children, and typical all-American lifestyle." She displayed her customary lifestyle and by doing so satisfied the conservative ideals of the Republican Party, and from there she discussed her family's love.

7. Comment on the speaker's delivery, evaluating all elements of voice, physical appearance, and movement.

The speaker used a manuscript as her vehicle to deliver her speech. Her body language gave the illusion the speech was extemporaneous; she spoke with deep emotion and delivered a sharp message.

Notes

1. Mary Fisher, "A Whisper of AIDS," *American Rhetoric*, August 12, 1992, accessed April 7, 2015. http://www.americanrhetoric.com/.

2. J. K. Barr, J.M. Waring, and L. J. Warshaw, "Knowledge and Attitudes about AIDS among Corporate and Public Service Employees," Am J Public Health, 1992 February; 82(2): 225–228, accessed April 9, 2015. http://www.ncbi.nlm.nih.gov/pmc/articles/PMC1694277/.

Robert F. Kennedy: Remarks on the Assassination of Martin Luther King Jr.

1. Levels of audience analysis:

On April 4, 1968, Robert F. Kennedy was on his way to Indianapolis to campaign for the Democratic presidential nomination when he heard that Martin Luther King had been shot. Senator Kennedy continued with his plans to attend the campaign rally located at Seventeenth and Broadway in Indianapolis's African American ghetto. Considering the demographics of the area in which he was to speak—low-income, high crime and little to no education—Senator Kennedy knew he had to gain the trust of his audience. His speech had to be effective in order to unify his audience and also support his efforts to win his campaign. I also observed how Senator Kennedy was able to use his speech about violence in order to connect with the emotions of his audience. He spoke of Martin Luther King's promotion of love, peace, and justice among all human beings. At the end of his speech, he convinces his audience that everyone wants social equality, asserting, "The great majority of white people … and black people want to live together." Senator Kennedy achieved his purpose by appealing to the audience that violence and more bloodshed was senseless. The crowd dispersed quietly instead of rioting, which took place in other cities.

Robert F. Kennedy's audience on the day of his speech, April 4, 1968, was predominately African Americans who lived in an area in Indianapolis considered the "ghetto." Members of minority groups generally live in these areas because of their social, legal, and/or economic status. Ghetto areas are usually rezoned, rehabilitated, and held out to be prime real estate, depending on their location. A few blocks from the area where Senator Kennedy stood on a platform in the back of a flatbed truck now stands a private elementary school, Oaks Academy. The school is apparently one of a kind: "97 percent of the 600 plus kids are proficient in both reading and math; 50 percent of the kids are on free or reduced lunch; almost 60 percent of the Oaks students are recipients of scholarships from the Indiana Opportunity Scholarship Program; and 50 percent of the kids come from middle- to upper-class families. Wealthy parents drive from as far away as Carmel, a well-to-do suburb, to enroll their kids in the school." Oaks Academy is just one example of how the demographics, cultures, and psychologies change in areas once considered ghettos.

Source

Chevous, Kevin. "Kennedy and King Dreamed of a Color-Blind Society." *Miami Times.* Jan. 28, 2015. Accessed: January 28, 2015. http://miamitimesonline.com/news/2015/jan/28/kennedy-and-king-dreamed-color-blind-society/?page=1.

2. The speaker's relationship to the audience:

Robert F. Kennedy appealed to his audience as Martin Luther King Jr. would have. He used the same words King dedicated his life to: love and justice. Senator Kennedy also appealed to his audience with the same nonviolence rhetoric King used in keeping peace among the people. He spoke against hate and revenge and convinced the people, instead of rioting, to go home and pray for King's family.

Robert F. Kennedy basically held the same values that King held in his beliefs that we should coexist harmoniously and not allow a tragic loss divide the nation against one another. Some of the major differences that would affect his *ethos* would be the fact that he was not of the same nationality as his audience. He was a white man, and a white man assassinated King. Despite his nobility and his beliefs and values, there was room for distrust in the African American community. He mentioned the death of his brother, John F. Kennedy, who also was murdered by a white man. He explained that hate was hate no matter the race, religion, or creed. Senator Kennedy's *ethos* was an appeal as a politician to his audience to not seek vengeance, hate, and bitterness. Senator Kennedy's *pathos* was the emotional appeal used by Martin Luther King's persuasion of love, peace and justice. His *logos* was the logical appeal in his persuasion to convince the people not to divide but stand together.

Martin Luther King Jr.'s death was a concern of Senator Kennedy's representatives and city officials. They feared for Senator Kennedy's safety, and there was the possibility of a riot once the message of King's death was delivered. But when the rally ended, the crowd dispersed quietly.

3. Identification:

I feel Robert Kennedy identified exceptionally well with his audience. If Senator Kennedy had not been received by his audience in the manner in which he was, there probably would have been a riot. Martin Luther King Jr. dedicated his life to love, peace, and justice, and Senator Kennedy identified with his audience by representing these same values. Senator Kennedy also identified with his audience in that he was trusted enough to convince them not to cause anymore senseless bloodshed in revenge for the assassination of their spiritual leader.

4. Overall performance:

Senator Kennedy's overall performance went very well with regard to his audience. His address was instrumental in convincing his audience not to seek revenge, for that approach would not be what King would have wanted.

Analyzing Our Audience

• What are the demographic characteristics of your audience?

My audience appears to be a mixture of students from several out-of-state locations, including Philadelphia, Pennsylvania. Their ages range from twenty to older, married with children, and some divorcees. There are also students in our military. The majority of students in my audience were in their second semester, some third year, and one graduating in May of this year.

• What values and beliefs do you believe you share in common with your audience?

The value I share in common with my audience is the appreciation of school, which I did not have when I was younger. It seems that the majority of students taking this course are returning to school to complete their education, realizing the need for a degree is essential in today's climate.

1. In three to four sentences, describe your audience's likely reaction to your midterm presentation topic. How will you make your topic relevant for your audience? What do you anticipate your audience will know about your topic?

    I believe my audience will react to my midterm presentation topic due to its content. Hopefully, I will be able to give my presentation on global warming and the effects it has on our climate. I would anticipate that my audience would know quite a bit about climate change because it is discussed on a daily basis, either on television or related to an occurrence involving our climate that has taken place in the world.

2. In three to four sentences, describe your audience's likely reaction to your final presentation topic. How will you make this topic interesting for your audience?

    The likely reaction to my final presentation topic should be quite interesting, as my audience will be quite familiar with the speakers. The three topics I listed as choices are "Hillary Clinton Discusses Empowering Women at CGI," "Obama State of the Union 2015 Address," and "President Bill Clinton: Yale University Class Day Speaker." I believe any one of the three topics listed will be of interest to my audience due to the speakers' credibility and contributions to our country as politicians.

Testing the Strength of Supporting Material

On December 11, 2007, former vice president Al Gore and the United Nations' Intergovernmental Panel on Global Warming and Climate Change were awarded the Nobel Peace Prize for their contributions in the war on global warming. Al Gore's primary purpose was to inform his audience about the negative effects of global warming—raising average global temperatures, and in turn melting glaciers, causing flooding, and drying up water masses, causing drought. Also, his purpose was to heighten awareness and increase responsiveness regarding the hazards of global warming and climate change.

The UN's Intergovernmental Panel on Climate Change brought together 2,500 researchers from more than 130 nations. The IPCC Fifth Assessment Report (AR5) provides an up-to-date view of current scientific knowledge relevant to climate change. The report consists of three working group reports and a synthesis report, which provides additional information regarding the outline and content and how the AR5 was prepared. Information about how the AR5 was prepared can be found at the website below.

"IPCC Intergovernmental Panel on Climate Change." *Fifth Assessment Report (AR5)*. Accessed February 7, 2015. http://ipcc.ch/.

Additional supportive information used in Gore's speech is the "September 21 report submitted by scientists with unprecedented alarm that the north polar ice cap is, in their words, 'falling off a cliff.'" Gore also used a study presented by US Navy researchers warning that the ice cap reference could happen within the next seven years.

The US Naval Research Laboratory is the Navy's full-spectrum corporate laboratory, conducting a broadly based multidisciplinary program of scientific research and advanced technological development. "Each year, the president recognizes and celebrates a group of senior career employees with the Presidential Rank Award." This year, the Honorable Robert O. Work, undersecretary of the Navy, presented the Presidential Rank Award to Dr. Judith Lean. "In 2004 to 2006, Dr. Lean served as lead author of a major section of the Intergovernmental Panel on Climate Change (IPCC) report, which resulted in her being awarded the Nobel Peace Prize as shared with Albert Gore and the IPCC."

Donna McKinney. "Dr. Judith Lean Receives Presidential Rank Award for Meritorious Senior Professional." *US Naval Research Laboratory*. Oct. 6, 2011. Accessed February 7, 2015. http://www.nrl.navy.mil/media/news-releases/2011/dr-judith-lean-receives-presidential-rank-award-for-meritorious-senior-professional.

Al Gore's Nobel speech clearly identifies his audience, and the supporting evidence used in his speech was, in my view, forthcoming. Gore's speech was intended to convince the listeners to adopt his framework, and in the process change their attitudes toward believing in climate change solutions. Shortly after his introduction, he describes how human pollution causes Earth to trap more heat. He makes the statement, "As a result, the Earth has a fever, and the fever is rising. A fever unchecked can lead to death. We are what is wrong, and we must make it right." I feel Gore could have elaborated more on deforestation, since he did mention how we are recklessly burning and clearing our forests and driving more species into extinction.

Albert A. Gore. "It's Time to Make Peace with the Planet"—Al Gore Accepts 2007 Nobel Peace Prize. *Democracy Now*. Dec. 11, 2007. Accessed February 5, 2015. http://www.democracynow.org/2007/12/11/it_is_time_to_make_peace.

Reasoning

Fallacies

Identify the fallacy in each of the following statements and, in each case, **briefly** explain *why* the statement is fallacious. Explain what kind of supporting material and reasoning you would use to make this claim valid.

1. It's ridiculous to worry about protecting America's national parks against pollution and overuse when innocent people are being killed by terrorists.

    False analogy: Things being compared have an important fundamental difference. American national parks and the protection against pollution and overuse have nothing to do with innocent people being killed by terrorists. Research the claim online and compare statistics as to how many people are being killed by terrorists.

2. There can be no doubt that the Great Depression was caused by Herbert Hoover. He became president in March 1929, and the stock market crashed just seven months later.

    Post hoc, ergo propter hoc: This fallacy assumes that if one event happens after another, the first must have caused the second. Although the stock market crashed roughly eight months after Herbert Hoover took office, it has not been proven that he caused the global economic slowdown (the Great Depression).

3. One nonsmoker interviewed at a restaurant said, "I can eat dinner just fine even though people around me are smoking." Another, responding to a *Los Angeles Times* survey, said, "I don't see what all the fuss is about. My wife has smoked for years, and it has never bothered me." We can see, then, that secondhand smoke does not cause a problem for most nonsmokers.

Hasty generalization: The size of the sample being used to reach the conclusion is too small to reach a certain conclusion. The two comparisons in this situation are not enough data to supply valid proof that smoke does not cause problems in most nonsmokers.

Testing the Strength of Supporting Material

Read and view Richard Nixon's "Checkers Speech," delivered in 1952. Then answer the following questions:

1. What was Nixon's primary purpose in the speech? Does the speech have more than one purpose? Provide evidence from the speech to support your claims.

The primary purpose in Nixon's speech was to convince his audience of his innocence regarding the $18,000 in campaign funds he was accused of using for his personal use. Senator Nixon, in his attempt to convince his audience he had done nothing wrong, diverts the audience's attention away from the issue at hand to topics unrelated to the subject, such as his appeal to our patriotic emotions by mentioning his military background and his association with service members. Nixon also describes where he came from as an additional ploy to divert his audience and convince them that he was just an average person:

> Our family was one of modest circumstances, and most of
> my early life was spent in a store out in East Whittier. It was
> a grocery store—one of those family enterprises. The only
> reason we were able to make it go was because my mother and
> dad had five boys, and we all worked in the store.

Richard Nixon. "Checkers Speech." September 23, 1952. Accessed February 25, 2015. http://millercenter.org/president/speeches/speech-4638.

2. Using the speech and the discussion, identify the following in Nixon's speech:

    a. **Claim.** If there is more than one claim, just choose one for this exercise.

    Senator Nixon's "Checkers Speech" was a ploy to convince the American people of his innocence in misappropriating campaign funds.

    b. **Supporting material** used to support the claim.

    A complete audit of Senator Nixon's campaign fund was produced to support his claim, along with a complete financial history of his earnings.

    c. Type of **reasoning** used to link the supporting material to the claim.

    The reasoning used to link the supporting material to the claim was the charges made against Senator Nixon questioning his honesty and integrity as to the misappropriation of campaign funds.

3. Do you recognize any reasoning fallacies in this speech? If so, identify the type of fallacy being committed and provide an example of each from the speech.

This is an example of the **straw man** fallacy, which consists of an attack on a view similar to but not the same as the one your opponent holds; it is a diversionary tactic. Another attempt of Nixon's to defend his reputation and to divert his audience was the mention of a pet dog given to his daughters.

> One other thing I probably should tell you, because if I don't they will probably be saying this about me, too. We did get something, a gift, after the election. A man down in Texas heard Pat on the radio mention the fact that our two youngsters would like to have a dog, and, believe it or not, the day before we left on this campaign trip we got a message from Union Station in Baltimore saying they had a package for us. We went

down to get it. You know what it was? It was a little cocker spaniel dog, in a crate that he had sent all the way from Texas, black-and-white, spotted, and our little girl, Tricia, the six-year-old, named it Checkers. And, you know, the kids, like all kids, loved the dog, and I just want to say this, right now, that regardless of what they say about it, we are going to keep it.

The issue here was the misappropriation of $18,000 of campaign funds, not the dog.

This is an example of a **false analogy**: An individual tries to explain difficult facts by making comparison by already known facts because of their similarity. He gives an example of a business matter he would facilitate for service member, which is a ploy to create confusion: "for example, when a constituent writes in and wants you to go down to the Veterans Administration and get some information about his GI policy."

Watch each of the *America Rocks!* segments, and then choose two to write about. In an essay of approximately three hundred to four hundred words, answer the following:

1. In these segments, what principles and values do the performances assume the audience shares? Go beyond the obvious here to discern what the underlying message is. Explain what led to your conclusions.

"Elbow Room"

My estimation of the underlying message is that the song and images are communicating a language that justified westward exploration—using the phrase "manifest destiny," which by its meaning gave white settlers the God-given right to expand their borders through exploration. If you noticed, the words "Oregon or bust" were spelled out on the covered wagons throughout the song, suggesting the determination these settlers had about going west. They were going to get there if it cost them their lives. The song mentions the many fights they had to win in order to gain land rights, and how the West was meant to be their manifest destiny. Unfortunately, the message wasn't complete in describing the types of fights that ensued, and how many Native Americans they slaughtered and starved to death by killing off their buffalo, which was their main source of food.

> In the 19ᵗʰ century US, Manifest Destiny was a belief that was widely held that the destiny of American settlers was to expand and move across the continent to spread their traditions and their institutions, while at the same time enlightening more primitive nations. And the American settlers of the time considered Indians and Hispanics to be inferior and therefore deserving of cultivation. The settlers considered the United States to be the best possible way to organize a country so they felt the need to remake the world in the image of their own country. Since they were sure of their cultural and racial superiority, they felt that their destiny was to spread their rule around and enlighten the nations that were not so lucky.[1]

The song "Elbow Room" has quite an interesting conclusion, as it implicates justification, by using the manifest destiny phrase, that the next land to be conquered is the moon and that Americans have the right to take possession in the same manner as the West.

"The Great American Melting Pot"

America is considered a melting pot in which people from around the world brought their cultures and practices then threw them into the American pot. Immigrants who migrated from their homeland to America were under the assumption that they were to leave their past cultures and practices behind and adapt to the new ways of America. True, the United States is culturally diverse, but immigrants became part of a dominant culture by giving up their true identity in order to fit into the mainstream of society.

> Historically, a more accurate metaphor is that the United States has a cultural "cookie-cutter" with a white, Anglo-Saxon, Protestant, male mold or shape. Immigrants who came to America from foreign countries learned English and changed their names so as to blend into the Protestant Christian communities. This process caused the ones that could fit into the cookie-cutter mold to advance quickly. Today the most economically successful are Arab Americans and Lebanese

Christians. American Indians, Mexican Americans, and African Americans were unable to fit the mold regardless of how much they acted like white Anglo-Saxon Protestants; they could not change the color of their skin or the texture of their hair. Mastering English and their mainstream values and behaviors, nonwhites were easily identifiably different and were easily excluded from the dominant culture.[2]

Is there a persuasive message to this production? If so, of what is it attempting to persuade the audience member? If not, what is its purpose? Again, go beyond the obvious.

It is my opinion and belief that there is not only a persuasive message to this production, but there is also a purpose, and that is to persuade the audience member through indoctrination. I will refer to this indoctrination as the "manifest destiny" indoctrination.

Indoctrination is the process of inculcating ideas, attitudes, cognitive strategies, or a professional methodology; it is a critical component in the transfer of cultures, customs, and traditions from one generation to the next. Some distinguish indoctrination from education, claiming that the indoctrinated person is not expected to question, or critically examine the doctrine they have learned.[3]

The manifest destiny indoctrination apparently won the hearts of white settlers, and one of its most critical components, racism, was transferred down through the generations. Perhaps this indoctrination was destined to be because the first Europeans who came to America in large numbers were not your typical Europeans. It is my understanding that many of them were fleeing Europe to avoid religious and political oppression, and the remainder were criminals who were sent to America by the British. Perhaps this indoctrination explains the settlers' ignorant and unethical way of thinking, which remains prevalent in America. For the past seven years, judging from the racism President Obama has experienced, and the families of young African-American men who have recently lost their lives due to police brutality, the future of this country for *all* people of color looks quite grim, to say the least. Criminals and radical religious fanatics, seriously! No wonder this country is in the state it's in!

2. What do you think of the appropriateness of airing these messages? Do they tell an accurate tale? Explain.

If these messages are to continue to air, which they probably will, the editors should go through them with a fine-toothed comb and add more truth to the productions. I think viewers of these productions should be taught the truth as far as how this country was really founded, or better yet, *stolen*. I've never understood how one discovers a country that is already inhabited. America was invaded by the settlers, not discovered.

3. Some of these productions are still being shown. In your opinion, do they still hold up? If you could remake the productions today, how might you change the content and style to adapt them to contemporary audiences?

These video clips are totally outdated and should be either removed from the Internet or edited with updated versions of the truth. Also, if I had the opportunity to remake the productions, I would certainly incorporate the *real* America in its present state. I would not have ignored the fact that there was a Native American presence in the Great Plains and on the West Coast at the time the settlers arrived in America. Nor would I have ignored the Chinese immigrants who contributed to our railroads across the country, and the participation of the Soviet Union in the Space Race. Nor would I have ignored the blood, sweat, and tears endured by my people being captured and enslaved in this country and treated like the animals they were not. And we continue to be discounted as a human race. The elimination of these facts was by far *no* accident.

View Barack Obama's "A More Perfect Union" address. In approximately two hundred to three hundred words, talk about the main values celebrated in this video, and what similarities and differences you observe between this video and the *America Rocks!* segments.

One of the main values celebrated in this video was Senator Obama's focus on family, as he proudly mentions he is the son of a black man from Kenya and a white woman from Kansas. The senator also tells the story of his white grandfather, who survived the Depression and served in World War II, and his white grandmother, who worked on an assembly line while his grandfather was overseas. He also mentions his wife, Michelle, a black American who carries the blood of slaves and slave owners, which was passed on to their two daughters.

Senator Obama also discusses his relationship with the Reverend Jeremiah Wright, and how he introduced the senator to his Christian faith. The senator's speech was made in response to the controversy over his connection to the reverend regarding statements made on American domestic and foreign policy and the treatment of African Americans. The senator discussed the values taught to him by the reverend (e.g., to care for the sick and lift up the poor) and how we are all obligated to love one another. He goes on to explain how the reverend strengthened his faith, officiated his wedding, and baptized his daughters.

The differences in the two videos are quite apparent. The *Schoolhouse Rock* videos have underlying subliminal racial messages. The settlers believed that their cultural and racial superiority gave them the God-given right through manifest destiny to remake the world. Barack Obama's "A More Perfect Union" address confronted the issues of race in America. The senator basically stated, "That racism has a sordid past in our history, it cannot be ignored, but must be confronted, discussed, and acted upon."

Make a list of five values you think contemporary American culture holds today. Where do you see these values expressed? How have cultural values changed since *America Rocks!*? Your answer should be approximately two hundred words.

Change: One value Americans see as a good condition; it is considered a link to progress, development, growth, and improvement.

Freedom: Freedom is the ability to believe whatever you choose and live as you choose as long as you harm no one else. Many believe that it is worth the time and possibly the loss of life to obtain it.

Democracy: A form of organized power wherein decisions are made by a vote.

Capitalism: Capitalism has made America great, but it generated its own set of inequalities.

Equality: Equality is a wonderful ideal—in fact, it is one of America's most cherished values. Unfortunately, there are large inequalities in economic and social resources, from wealth and income to education and social status.

One very important value I feel has changed over the years is that of communication and personal interaction between each other. Social media, along with cell phones and the Internet, has basically caused the decline in communication among families, both children and parents. A recent study found that, due to technology, a "new connectedness" is being created by parents with their children, but as a consequence, old habits are disappearing. Internet browsing is replacing the once family activity of television watching as a group. Before technology, families shared meals at the dining room table, and discussed their days at work and school. People communicated with each other! Newspapers were read, and if there was something that needed researching, we went to the library. Technology has taken the place of in-person communication. There has also been a decline in family values, such as marriage; divorces are more common now as opposed to "back in the day." Our children have lost respect not only for their parents, but for our schoolteachers and people of authority.

"Although Americans may think of themselves as being more varied and unpredictable than they actually are, it is significant that they think they are. Americans tend to think they have been only slightly influenced by family, church, or schools. In the end, each believes, 'I personally chose which values I want to live my own life by.'"[4]

Notes

1. "Historynet.com," *Manifest Destiny*, Accessed March 31, 2015, http://www.historynet.com/manifest-destiny.

2. "Gary R. Weaver, PhD," *American Cultural Values*, Accessed March 31, 2015, http://trends.gmfus.org/doc/mmf/American%20Cultural%20Values.pdf.

3. "Wikipedia: The Free Encyclopedia," February 5, 2015, Accessed April 1, 2015, http://en.wikipedia.org/wiki/Indoctrination.

4. "L. Robert Kohls, PhD," *The Values Americans Live By,* Reprinted 1988, Accessed April 2, 2015, http://www.sba.pdx.edu/faculty/amlei/alaccess/576/ValuesAmericansLiveBy.pdf.

PROPOSALS

Workers without Borders

1. Jennifer Gordon defines the problem in her opening statement: "Americans are hardly in the mood to welcome new immigrants." She assumes her readers are aware of the reason for the problem, which is undocumented workers providing labor to employers in all areas of our industry, and the situation causing competition and increasing job scarcity in the United States. She also notes that there is an urgent need for immigration reform, and assumes that her readers are sympathetic to the problems with undocumented workers. I agree with her assumption that there should be immigration reform and that immigrants should have the same rights and equality in the workplace as Americans.

2. Ms. Gordon's reasoning is that the current system is hurting working conditions and wages for everyone. She feels that if a plan was put into effect to allow the undocumented workers to be brought into the United States for agricultural and seasonal jobs by joining workers' organizations, like Transnational Labor Citizenship, it would allow employers access to more workers, but on fair terms. The policies that support free trade in goods and jobs would be addressed, along with the inhumanity and inconsistencies within these policies. This plan would also allow illegal immigrants the opportunity to become citizens.

3. One objection would be the lack of jobs in this country today, and the fact that immigrants will work for cheaper wages, which in turn causes fewer jobs for Americans and rising unemployment. I agree with Ms. Gordon that the United States needs an open and fair system, but for some reason we cannot seem to get one in place.

Support and Pass the California Dream Act

1. Monica Balmelli's reasons for signing the petition are the suicides and slavery conditions at the Apple factories in China. Foxconn is the manufacturer of Apple, Inc., in China, where workers are subjected to unlawful and dehumanizing working conditions. They have a high suicide rate; workers jump to their deaths because of exhaustion and being overworked.

2. The difference in appeal between the two petitions is that in "Tell Apple" the signers are identified as consumers and as Apple users and lovers. This appeal enables Apple to match the quality of its design with the quality of working conditions for those responsible in the production of Apple's products. On the other hand, "Support and Pass the California Dream Act" identifies the signer as "we, the undersigned," which represents businesses, civic, legal, religious, and educational groups and institutions that support the act.

3. The undocumented students are portrayed in the "Dream Act" petition as hardworking, bright students who one day may aspire to and become teachers, politicians, and so forth. They are also portrayed as hardworking immigrant youths who are student body presidents, honor students, outstanding athletes and community leaders, and aspiring professionals who wish to complete a higher education. The urgency with the Foxconn petition is the asking for a remedy concerning the labor conditions at their facility in China. There should be the same quality in their working conditions as there is in the production of their products.

Analysis: Developing a Solution

Jennifer Gordon's proposal for a transnational organization of workers without borders starts with a problem that many Americans will recognize immediately—namely, that undocumented workers are providing the labor for employers in the United States in agriculture, construction, gardening, hotels, restaurants, meat packing, manufacturing, and other industries. She doesn't spend much time laying out the problem, aside from noting that it "traps migrants in bad jobs and ends up lowering wages all around." Her focus, rather, is on the solution and how to implement it. To make her case for migrant mobility, she cites the experience of the European Union. This is meant to be reassuring in that the influx of migrant workers did not lower native workers' wages or limit their employment. But in a key rhetorical move, she also concedes problems, in that some workers "were cheated on their wages and worked in unsafe conditions." Notice how this sets her up to make a refinement in her proposal by saying that workplace protection, as well as mobility, is a crucial part of her proposal.

Objectives

Upon completion of this material, the student should be able to

- understand the basic characteristic of the rhetorical situation;

- apply rhetorical concepts to the analysis of a short piece of writing;

- grasp how writers use rhetorical appeals—ethos, pathos, and logos—in combination in order to adopt a stance that is appropriate to a rhetorical situation; and

- identify the strategies used to write a rhetorical analysis: close reading, description of the text, explanation of the background of the text, and interpretation of a writer's rhetorical choices.

---

1   Barbara Garson is the author of a series of books describing American working lives at historical turning points, including *All the Livelong Day* (1975), *The Electronic Sweatshop* (1988), and *Money Makes the World Go Around* (2001). Her new book, just published, is <u>*Down the Up Escalator: How the 99% Live in the Great Recession*</u> (Doubleday). <u>www.TheNation.com</u>.

Printed in the United States
By Bookmasters